W.B. WALKER.

£2-50

The Family Reunion

by T. S. Eliot

verse
COLLECTED POEMS, 1909–1935
FOUR QUARTETS
THE CULTIVATION OF CHRISTMAS TREES

selected verse
SELECTED POEMS
THE WASTE LAND

children's verse
OLD POSSUM'S BOOK OF PRACTICAL CATS

plays
COLLECTED PLAYS
MURDER IN THE CATHEDRAL
THE FAMILY REUNION
THE COCKTAIL PARTY
THE CONFIDENTIAL CLERK
THE ELDER STATESMAN

literary criticism
SELECTED ESSAYS
THE USE OF POETRY AND THE
USE OF CRITICISM
ON POETRY AND POETS

social criticism
THE IDEA OF A CHRISTIAN SOCIETY
NOTES TOWARDS THE DEFINITION OF CULTURE

philosophy
KNOWLEDGE AND EXPERIENCE:
in the Philosophy of F. H. Bradley

selected prose
SELECTED PROSE (with Penguin Books Ltd.)

film script
THE FILM OF MURDER IN THE CATHEDRAL

translation
ANABASIS a poem by St.-John Perse

THE
FAMILY REUNION

a play by

T. S. ELIOT

W. B. Walker VI

FABER AND FABER LTD
24 Russell Square
London

First published in mcmxxxix
by Faber and Faber Limited
24 Russell Square London W.C.1
First published in this edition mcmlxiii
Printed in Great Britain by
R. MacLehose and Company Limited
The University Press Glasgow
All rights reserved

Persons

AMY, DOWAGER LADY MONCHENSEY

IVY, VIOLET, *and* AGATHA, *her younger sisters*

COL. THE HON. GERALD PIPER, *and* THE HON. CHARLES PIPER, *brothers of her deceased husband*

MARY, *daughter of a deceased cousin of Lady Monchensey*

DENMAN, *a parlourmaid*

HARRY, LORD MONCHENSEY, *Amy's eldest son*

DOWNING, *his servant and chauffeur*

DR. WARBURTON

SERGEANT WINCHELL

THE EUMENIDES

The scene is laid in a country house in the North of England

7

Part I

The Drawing Room, after Tea
An afternoon in late March

Aristotle's "Unities?"

1) Scenes must take place in widely
   divergent places.
2) 1 plot — unity of subj.
3) must take place within 12 hrs.

Shakespeare bust them.

Scene I

AMY

Not yet! I will ring for you. It is still quite light.
I have nothing to do but watch the days draw out,
Now that I sit in the house from October to June,
And the swallow comes too soon and the spring will be
    over
And the cuckoo will be gone before I am out again.
O Sun, that was once so warm, O Light that was taken for
    granted
When I was young and strong, and sun and light unsought
    for
And the night unfeared and the day expected
And clocks could be trusted, tomorrow assured
And time would not stop in the dark!
Put on the lights. But leave the curtains undrawn.
Make up the fire. Will the spring never come? I am cold.

AGATHA

Wishwood was always a cold place, Amy.

11

IVY

I have always told Amy she should go south in the winter.
Were I in Amy's position, I would go south in the winter.
I would follow the sun, not wait for the sun to come here.
I would go south in the winter, if I could afford it,
Not freeze, as I do, in Bayswater, by a gas-fire counting
     shillings.

VIOLET

Go south! to the English circulating libraries,
To the military widows and the English chaplains,
To the chilly deck-chair and the strong cold tea —
The strong cold stewed bad Indian tea.

CHARLES

That's not Amy's style at all. We are country-bred people.
Amy has been too long used to our ways
Living with horses and dogs and guns
Ever to want to leave England in the winter.
But a single man like me is better off in London:
A man can be very cosy at his club
Even in an English winter.

GERALD

        Well, as for me,
I'd just as soon be a subaltern again
To be back in the East. An incomparable climate
For a man who can exercise a little common prudence;
And your servants look after you very much better.

AMY

My servants are perfectly competent, Gerald.
I can still see to that.

VIOLET

Well, as for me,
I would never go south, no, definitely never,
Even could I do it as well as Amy:
England's bad enough, I would never go south,
Simply to see the vulgarest people —
You can keep out of their way at home;
People with money from heaven knows where —

GERALD

Dividends from aeroplane shares.

VIOLET

They bathe all day and they dance all night
In the absolute *minimum* of clothes.

CHARLES

It's the cocktail-drinking does the harm:
There's nothing on earth so bad for the young.
All that a civilised person needs
Is a glass of dry sherry or two before dinner.
The modern young people don't know what they're drinking,
Modern young people don't care what they're eating;
They've lost their sense of taste and smell
Because of their cocktails and cigarettes.
[*Enter* DENMAN *with sherry and whisky.* CHARLES *takes
    sherry and* GERALD *whisky.*]
That's what it comes to.
                    [*Lights a cigarette*]

IVY

The younger generation
Are undoubtedly decadent.

13

CHARLES

                  The younger generation
Are not what we were. Haven't the stamina,
Haven't the sense of responsibility.

GERALD

You're being very hard on the younger generation.
I don't come across them very much now, myself;
But I must say I've met some very decent specimens
And some first-class shots — better than you were,
Charles, as I remember. Besides, you've got to make
        allowances:
We haven't left them such an easy world to live in.
Let the younger generation speak for itself:
It's Mary's generation. What does she think about it?

MARY

Really, Cousin Gerald, if you want information
About the younger generation, you must ask someone else.
I'm afraid that I don't deserve the compliment:
I don't belong to any generation.

                                        [*Exit*]

VIOLET

Really, Gerald, I must say you're very tactless,
And I think that Charles might have been more con-
        siderate.

GERALD

I'm very sorry: but why was she upset?
I only meant to draw her into the conversation.

CHARLES

She's a nice girl; but it's a difficult age for her.

I suppose she must be getting on for thirty?
She ought to be married, that's what it is.

AMY

So she should have been, if things had gone as I intended.
Harry's return does not make things easy for her
At the moment: but life may still go right.
Meanwhile, let us drop the subject. The less said the better.

GERALD

That reminds me, Amy,
When are the boys all due to arrive?

AMY

I do not want the clock to stop in the dark.
If you want to know why I never leave Wishwood
That is the reason. I keep Wishwood alive
To keep the family alive, to keep them together,
To keep me alive, and I live to keep them.
You none of you understand how old you are
And death will come to you as a mild surprise,
A momentary shudder in a vacant room.
Only Agatha seems to discover some meaning in death
Which I cannot find.
— I am only certain of Arthur and John,
Arthur in London, John in Leicestershire:
They should both be here in good time for dinner.
Harry telephoned to me from Marseilles,
He would come by air to Paris, and so to London,
And hoped to arrive in the course of the evening.

VIOLET

Harry was always the most likely to be late.

15

AMY

This time, it will not be his fault.
We are very lucky to have Harry at all.

IVY

And when will you have your birthday cake, Amy,
And open your presents?

AMY
After dinner:
That is the best time.

IVY
It is the first time
You have not had your cake and your presents at tea.

AMY

This is a very particular occasion
As you ought to know. It will be the first time
For eight years that we have all been together.

AGATHA

It is going to be rather painful for Harry
After eight years and all that has happened
To come back to Wishwood.

GERALD
Why, painful?

VIOLET
Gerald! you know what Agatha means.

16

AGATHA

I mean painful, because everything is irrevocable,
Because the past is irremediable,
Because the future can only be built
Upon the real past. Wandering in the tropics
Or against the painted scene of the Mediterranean,
Harry must often have remembered Wishwood —
The nursery tea, the school holiday,
The daring feats on the old pony,
And thought to creep back through the little door.
He will find a new Wishwood. Adaptation is hard.

AMY

Nothing is changed, Agatha, at Wishwood.
Everything is kept as it was when he left it,
Except the old pony, and the mongrel setter
Which I had to have destroyed.
Nothing has been changed. I have seen to that.

AGATHA

Yes. I mean that at Wishwood he will find another
    Harry.
The man who returns will have to meet
The boy who left. Round by the stables,
In the coach-house, in the orchard,
In the plantation, down the corridor
That led to the nursery, round the corner
Of the new wing, he will have to face him —
And it will not be a very *jolly* corner.
When the loop in time comes — and it does not come for
    everybody —
The hidden is revealed, and the spectres show themselves.

17

I don't in the least know what you're talking about.
You seem to be wanting to give us all the hump.
I must say, this isn't cheerful for Amy's birthday
Or for Harry's homecoming. Make him feel at home, I say!
Make him feel that what has happened doesn't matter.
He's taken his medicine, I've no doubt.
Let him marry again and carry on at Wishwood.

AMY

Thank you, Gerald. Though Agatha means
As a rule, a good deal more than she cares to betray,
I am bound to say that I agree with you.

CHARLES

I never wrote to him when he lost his wife
That was just about a year ago, wasn't it?
Do you think I ought to mention it now?
It seems to me too late.

AMY

Much too late.
If he wants to talk about it, that's another matter;
But I don't believe he will. He will wish to forget it.
I do not mince matters in front of the family:
You can call it nothing but a blessed relief.

VIOLET

I call it providential.

IVY

Yet it must have been shocking,
Especially to lose anybody in *that* way —

18

Swept off the deck in the middle of a storm,
And never even to recover the body.

CHARLES

'Well-known Peeress Vanishes from Liner'.

GERALD

Yes, it's odd to think of her as permanently *missing*.

VIOLET

Had she been drinking?

AMY

I would never ask him.

IVY

These things are much better not enquired into.
She may have done it in a fit of temper.

GERALD

I never met her.

AMY

I am very glad you did not.
I am very glad that none of you ever met her.
It will make the situation very much easier
And is why I was so anxious you should all be here.
She never would have been one of the family,
She never wished to be one of the family,
She only wanted to keep him to herself
To satisfy her vanity. That's why she dragged him
All over Europe and half round the world
To expensive hotels and undesirable society

19

Which she could choose herself. She never wanted
Harry's relations or Harry's old friends;
She never wanted to fit herself to Harry,
But only to bring Harry down to her own level.
A restless shivering painted shadow
In life, she is less than a shadow in death.
You might as well all of you know the truth
For the sake of the future. There can be no grief
And no regret and no remorse.
I would have prevented it if I could. For the sake of the
        future:
Harry is to take command at Wishwood
And I hope we can contrive his future happiness.
Do not discuss his absence. Please behave only
As if nothing had happened in the last eight years.

GERALD

That will be a little difficult.

VIOLET
                Nonsense, Gerald!
You must see for yourself it's the only thing to do.

AGATHA

Thus with most careful devotion
Thus with precise attention
To detail, interfering preparation
Of that which is already prepared
Men tighten the knot of confusion
Into perfect misunderstanding,
Reflecting a pocket-torch of observation
Upon each other's opacity

Neglecting all the admonitions
From the world around the corner
The wind's talk in the dry holly-tree
The inclination of the moon
The attraction of the dark passage
The paw under the door.

CHORUS N.B. *hark-back to Greek drag.*
(IVY, VIOLET, GERALD *and* CHARLES)

Why do we feel embarrassed, impatient, fretful, ill at ease,

Assembled like amateur actors who have not been assigned
their parts?

Like amateur actors in a dream when the curtain rises, to
find themselves dressed for a different play, or having
rehearsed the wrong parts,

Waiting for the rustling in the stalls, the titter in the dress
circle, the laughter and catcalls in the gallery?

CHARLES

I might have been in St. James's Street, in a comfortable
chair rather nearer the fire.

IVY

I might have been visiting Cousin Lily at Sidmouth, if I had
not had to come to this party.

GERALD

I might have been staying with Compton-Smith, down at
his place in Dorset.

VIOLET

I should have been helping Lady Bumpus, at the Vicar's
American Tea.

21

CHORUS

Yet we are here at Amy's command, to play an unread part
    in some monstrous farce, ridiculous in some nightmare
    pantomime.

AMY

What's that? I thought I saw someone pass the window.
What time is it?

CHARLES

Nearly twenty to seven.

AMY

John should be here now, he has the shortest way to come.
John at least, if not Arthur. Hark, there is someone coming:
Yes, it must be John.
[*Enter* HARRY]

        Harry!
[HARRY *stops suddenly at the door and stares at the window*]

IVY

Welcome, Harry!

GERALD

Well done!

VIOLET

Welcome home to Wishwood!

CHARLES

Why, what's the matter?

AMY

Harry, if you want the curtains drawn you should let me
    ring for Denman.

22

HARRY

How can you sit in this blaze of light for all the world to
   look at?
If you knew how you looked, when I saw you through the
   window!
Do you like to be stared at by eyes through a window?

AMY

You forget, Harry, you are at Wishwood,
Not in town, where you have to close the blinds.
There is no one to see you but our servants who belong here,
And who all want to see you back, Harry.

HARRY

Look there, look there: do you see them?

GERALD

No, I don't see anyone about.

HARRY

                         No, no, not there. Look there!
Can't you see them? *You* don't see them, but I see them,
And they see me. This is the first time that I have seen
   them.
In the Java Straits, in the Sunda Sea,
In the sweet sickly tropical night, I knew they were
   coming.
In Italy, from behind the nightingale's thicket,
The eyes stared at me, and corrupted that song.
Behind the palm trees in the Grand Hotel
They were always there. But I did not *see* them.
Why should they wait until I came back to Wishwood?

There were a thousand places where I might have met
    them!
Why here? why here?

                Many happy returns of the day, mother.
Aunt Ivy, Aunt Violet, Uncle Gerald, Uncle Charles, Agatha.

AMY

We are very glad to have you back, Harry.
Now we shall all be together for dinner.
The servants have been looking forward to your coming:
Would you like to have them in after dinner
Or wait till tomorrow? I am sure you must be tired.
You will find everybody here, and everything the same.
Mr. Bevan — you remember — wants to call tomorrow
On some legal business, a question about taxes —
But I think you would rather wait till you are rested.
Your room is all ready for you. Nothing has been changed.

HARRY

Changed? nothing changed? how can you say that nothing
    is changed?
You all look so withered and young.

GERALD

             We must have a ride tomorrow.
You'll find you know the country as well as ever.
There wasn't an inch of it you didn't know.
But you'll have to see about a couple of new hunters.

CHARLES

And I've a new wine merchant to recommend you;
Your cellar could do with a little attention.

IVY

And you'll really have to find a successor to old Hawkins.
It's really high time the old man was pensioned.
He's let the rock garden go to rack and ruin,
And he's nearly half blind. I've spoken to your mother
Time and time again: she's done nothing about it
Because she preferred to wait for your coming.

VIOLET

And time and time again I have spoken to your mother
About the waste that goes on in the kitchen.
Mrs. Packell is too old to know what she is doing.
It really needs a man in charge of things at Wishwood.

AMY

You see your aunts and uncles are very helpful, Harry.
I have always found them forthcoming with advice
Which I have never taken. Now it is your business.
I have only struggled to keep Wishwood going
And to make no changes before your return.
Now it's for you to manage. I am an old woman.
They can give me no further advice when I'm dead.

IVY

Oh, dear Amy!
No one wants you to die, I'm sure!
Now that Harry's back, is the time to think of living.

HARRY

Time and time and time, and change, no change!
You all of you try to talk as if nothing had happened,
And yet you are talking of nothing else. Why not get to the
    point

Or if you want to pretend that I am another person —
A person that you have conspired to invent, please do so
In my absence. I shall be less embarrassing to you. Agatha?

AGATHA

I think, Harry, that having got so far —
If you want no pretences, let us have no pretences:
And you must try at once to make us understand,
And we must try to understand you.

HARRY

But how can I explain, how can I explain to *you*?
You will understand less after I have explained it.
All that I could hope to make you understand
Is only events: not what has happened.
And people to whom nothing has ever happened
Cannot understand the unimportance of events.

GERALD

Well, you can't say that nothing has happened to *me*.
I started as a youngster on the North-West Frontier —
Been in tight corners most of my life
And some pretty nasty messes.

CHARLES

And there isn't much would surprise me, Harry;
Or shock me, either.

HARRY

You are all people
To whom nothing has happened, at most a continual impact
Of external events. You have gone through life in sleep,

Never woken to the nightmare. I tell you, life would be
    unendurable
If you were wide awake. You do not know
The noxious smell untraceable in the drains,
Inaccessible to the plumbers, that has its hour of the night;
    you do not know
The unspoken voice of sorrow in the ancient bedroom
At three o'clock in the morning. I am not speaking
Of my own experience, but trying to give you
Comparisons in a more familiar medium. I am the old house
With the noxious smell and the sorrow before morning,
In which all past is present, all degradation
Is unredeemable. As for what happens —
Of the past you can only see what is past,
Not what is always present. That is what matters.

AGATHA

Nevertheless, Harry, best tell us as you can:
Talk in your own language, without stopping to debate
Whether it may be too far beyond our understanding.

HARRY

The sudden solitude in a crowded desert
In a thick smoke, many creatures moving
Without direction, for no direction
Leads anywhere but round and round in that vapour —
Without purpose, and without principle of conduct
In flickering intervals of light and darkness;
The partial anæsthesia of suffering without feeling
And partial observation of one's own automatism
While the slow stain sinks deeper through the skin
Tainting the flesh and discolouring the bone —

27

This is what matters, but it is unspeakable,
Untranslatable: I talk in general terms
Because the particular has no language. One thinks to
    escape
By violence, but one is still alone
In an over-crowded desert, jostled by ghosts.
It was only reversing the senseless direction
For a momentary rest on the burning wheel
That cloudless night in the mid-Atlantic
When I pushed her over.

VIOLET
Pushed her?

HARRY
You would never imagine anyone could sink so quickly.
I had always supposed, wherever I went
That she would be with me; whatever I did
That she was unkillable. It was not like that.
Everything is true in a different sense.
I expected to find her when I went back to the cabin.
Later, I became excited, I think I made enquiries;
The purser and the steward were extremely sympathetic
And the doctor very attentive.
That night I slept heavily, alone.

AMY
Harry!

CHARLES
You mustn't indulge such dangerous fancies.
It's only doing harm to your mother and yourself.

28

Of course we know what really happened, we read it in the
      papers —
No need to revert to it. Remember, my boy,
I understand, your life together made it seem more horrible.
There's a lot in my own past life that presses on my chest
When I wake, as I do now, early before morning.
I understand these feelings better than you know —
But *you* have no reason to reproach yourself.
Your conscience can be clear.

HARRY

                    It goes a good deal deeper
Than what people call their conscience; it is just the cancer
That eats away the self. I knew how you would take it.
First of all, you isolate the single event
As something so dreadful that it couldn't have happened,
Because you could not bear it. So you must believe
That I suffer from delusions. It is not my conscience,
Not my mind, that is diseased, but the world I have to live
      in.
— I lay two days in contented drowsiness;
Then I recovered. I am afraid of sleep:
A condition in which one can be caught for the last time.
And also waking. She is nearer than ever.
The contamination has reached the marrow
And *they* are always near. Here, nearer than ever.
They are very close here. I had not expected that.

AMY

Harry, Harry, you are very tired
And overwrought. Coming so far
And making such haste, the change is too sudden for you.

29

You are unused to our foggy climate
And the northern country. When you see Wishwood
Again by day, all will be the same again.
I beg you to go now and rest before dinner.
Get Downing to draw you a hot bath,
And you will feel better.

AGATHA

There are certain points I do not yet understand:
They will be clear later. I am also convinced
That you only hold a fragment of the explanation.
It is only because of what you do not understand
That you feel the need to declare what you do.
There is more to understand: hold fast to that
As the way to freedom.

HARRY

I think I see what you mean,
Dimly — as you once explained the sobbing in the chimney
The evil in the dark closet, which they said was not there,
Which they explained away, but you explained them
Or at least, made me cease to be afraid of them.
I will go and have my bath.

[Exit]

GERALD

God preserve us!
I never thought it would be as bad as this.

VIOLET

There is only one thing to be done:
Harry must see a doctor.

IVY

But I understand —
I have heard of such cases before — that people in his con-
    dition
Often betray the most immoderate resentment
At such a suggestion. They can be very cunning —
Their malady makes them so. They do not want to be cured
And they know what you are thinking.

CHARLES

He has probably let this notion grow in his mind,
Living among strangers, with no one to talk to.
I suspect it is simply that the wish to get rid of her
Makes him believe he did. He cannot trust his good
    fortune.
I believe that all he needs is someone to talk to,
To get it off his mind. I'll have a talk to him tomorrow.

AMY

Most certainly not, Charles, you are not the right person.
I prefer to believe that a few days at Wishwood
Among his own family, is all that he needs.

GERALD

Nevertheless, Amy, there's something in Violet's sug-
    gestion.
Why not ring up Warburton, and ask him to join us?
He's an old friend of the family, it's perfectly natural
That he should be asked. He looked after all the boys
When they were children. I'll have a word with him.
He can talk to Harry, and Harry need have no suspicion.
I'd trust Warburton's opinion.

AMY

If anyone speaks to Dr. Warburton
It should be myself. What does Agatha think?

AGATHA

It seems a necessary move
In an unnecessary action,
Not for the good that it will do
But that nothing may be left undone
On the margin of the impossible.

AMY

Very well.
I will ring up the doctor myself.

[*Exit*]

CHARLES

Meanwhile, I have an idea. Why not question Downing?
He's been with Harry ten years, he's absolutely discreet.
He was with them on the boat. He might be of use.

IVY

Charles! you don't really suppose
That he might have pushed her over?

CHARLES

In any case, I shouldn't blame Harry.
I might have done the same thing once, myself
Nobody knows what he's likely to do
Until there's somebody he wants to get rid of.

GERALD

Even so, we don't want Downing to know

Any more than he knows already.
And even if he knew, it's very much better
That he shouldn't know that we knew it also.
Why not let sleeping dogs lie?

CHARLES

All the same, there's a question or two
                    [*Rings the bell*]
That I'd like to ask Downing.

                    He shan't know why I'm asking.
[*Enter* DENMAN]
Denman, where is Downing? Is he up with his Lordship?

DENMAN

He's out in the garage, Sir, with his Lordship's car.

CHARLES

Tell him I'd like to have a word with him, please.
                    [*Exit* DENMAN]

VIOLET

Charles, if you are determined upon this investigation,
Which I am convinced is going to lead us nowhere,
And which I am sure Amy would disapprove of —
I only wish to express my emphatic protest
Both against your purpose and the means you are em-
      ploying.

CHARLES

My purpose is, to find out what's wrong with Harry:
Until we know that, we can do nothing for him.
And as for my means, we can't afford to be squeamish

In taking hold of anything that comes to hand.
If you are interested in helping Harry
You can hardly object to the means.

CENTER
VIOLET

I do object.

CENTER
IVY

And I wish to associate myself with my sister
In her objections —

CENTER
AGATHA

I have no objection,
Any more than I object to asking Dr. Warburton:
I only see that this is all quite irrelevant;
We had better leave Charles to talk to Downing
And pursue his own methods.

                                    [*Rises*]

CENTER
VIOLET

I do not agree.
I think there should be witnesses. I intend to remain.
And I wish to be present to hear what Downing says.
I want to know at once, not be told about it later.

CENTER
IVY

And I shall stay with Violet.

CENTER
AGATHA

I shall return
When Downing has left you.

                                    [*Exit*]

CHARLES

Well, I'm very sorry
You all see it like this: but there simply are times
When there's nothing to do but take the bull by the horns,
And this is one.

[*Knock: and enter* DOWNING]

CHARLES

Good evening, Downing.
It's good to see you again, after all these years.
You're well, I hope?

DOWNING

Thank you, very well indeed, Sir.

CHARLES

I'm sorry to send for you so abruptly,
But I've a question I'd like to put to you,
I'm sure you won't mind, it's about his Lordship.
You've looked after his Lordship for over ten years . . .

DOWNING

Eleven years, Sir, next Lady Day.

CHARLES

Eleven years, and you know him pretty well.
And I'm sure that you've been a good friend to him, too.
We haven't seen him for nearly eight years;
And to tell the truth, now that we've seen him,
We're a little worried about his health.
He doesn't seem to be . . . quite himself.

35

DOWNING

Quite natural, if I may say so, Sir,
After what happened.

CHARLES

Quite so, quite.
Downing, you were with them on the voyage from New
     York —
We didn't learn very much about the circumstances;
We only knew what we read in the papers —
Of course, there was a great deal too much in the papers.
Downing, do you think that it might have been suicide,
And that his Lordship knew it?

DOWNING

Unlikely, Sir, if I may say so.
Much more likely to have been an accident.
I mean, knowing her Ladyship,
I don't think she had the courage.

CHARLES

Did she ever talk of suicide?

DOWNING

Oh yes, she did, every now and again.
But in my opinion, it is those that talk
That are the least likely. To my way of thinking
She only did it to frighten people.
If you take my meaning — just for the effect.

CHARLES

I understand, Downing. Was she in good spirits?

DOWNING

Well, always about the same, Sir.
What I mean is, always up and down.
Down in the morning, and up in the evening,
And *then* she used to get rather excited,
And, in a way, irresponsible, Sir.
If I may make so bold, Sir,
I always thought that a very few cocktails
Went a long way with her Ladyship.
She wasn't one of those that are *designed* for drinking:
It's natural for some and unnatural for others.

CHARLES

And how was his Lordship, during the voyage?

DOWNING

Well, you might say depressed, Sir.
But you know his Lordship was always very quiet:
Very uncommon that I saw him in high spirits.
For what my judgment's worth, I always said his Lordship
Suffered from what they call a kind of repression.
But what struck me . . . more nervous than usual;
I mean to say, you could see that he was nervous.
He behaved as if he thought something might happen.

CHARLES

What sort of thing?

DOWNING

Well, I don't know, Sir.
But he seemed very anxious about my Lady.
Tried to keep her in when the weather was rough,

Didn't like to see her lean over the rail.
He was in a rare fright, once or twice.
But you know, it is just my opinion, Sir,
That his Lordship is rather psychic, as they say.

CHARLES

Were they always together?

DOWNING

Always, Sir.
That was just my complaint against my Lady.
It's my opinion that man and wife
Shouldn't see too much of each other, Sir.
Quite the contrary of the usual opinion,
I dare say. She wouldn't leave him alone.
And there's my complaint against these ocean liners
With all their swimming baths and gymnasiums
There's not even a place where a man can go
For a quiet smoke, where the women can't follow him.
She wouldn't leave him out of her sight.

CHARLES

During that evening, did you see him?

DOWNING

Oh yes, Sir, I'm sure I saw him.
I don't mean to say that he had any orders —
His Lordship is always most considerate
About keeping me up. But when I say I saw him,
I mean that I saw him accidental.
You see, Sir, I was down in the Tourist,
And I took a bit of air before I went to bed,

And you could see the corner of the upper deck.
And I remember, there I saw his Lordship
Leaning over the rail, looking at the water —
There wasn't a moon, but I was sure it was him.
While I took my turn about, for near half an hour
He stayed there alone, looking over the rail.
Her Ladyship must have been all right then,
Mustn't she, Sir? or else he'd have known it.

CHARLES

Oh yes . . . quite so. Thank you, Downing,
I don't think we need you any more.

GERALD

Oh, Downing,
Is there anything wrong with his Lordship's car?

DOWNING

Oh no, Sir, she's in good running order:
I see to that.

GERALD

I only wondered
Why you've been busy about it tonight.

DOWNING

Nothing wrong, Sir:
Only I like to have her always ready.
Would there be anything more, Sir?

GERALD

Thank you, Downing;
Nothing more.

[*Exit* DOWNING]

VIOLET

Well, Charles, I must say, with your investigations,
You seem to have left matters much as they were —
Except for having brought Downing into it:
Of which I disapprove.

CHARLES

                    Of which you disapprove.
But I believe that an unconscious accomplice is desirable.

CHORUS

Why should we stand here like guilty conspirators, waiting
      for some revelation
When the hidden shall be exposed, and the newsboy shall
      shout in the street?
When the private shall be made public, the common photo-
      grapher
Flashlight for the picture papers: why do we huddle to-
      gether
In a horrid amity of misfortune? why should we be impli-
      cated, brought in and brought together?

IVY

I do not trust Charles with his confident vulgarity, acquired
      from worldly associates.

GERALD

Ivy is only concerned for herself, and her credit among her
      shabby genteel acquaintance.

VIOLET

Gerald is certain to make some blunder, he is useless out of
      the army.

CHARLES

Violet is afraid that her status as Amy's sister will be
    diminished.

CHORUS

We all of us make the pretension
To be the uncommon exception
To the universal bondage.
We like to appear in the newspapers
So long as we are in the right column.
We know about the railway accident
We know about the sudden thrombosis
And the slowly hardening artery.
We like to be thought well of by others
So that we may think well of ourselves.
And any explanation will satisfy:
We only ask to be reassured
About the noises in the cellar
And the window that should not have been open.
Why do we all behave as if the door might suddenly open,
    the curtains be drawn,
The cellar make some dreadful disclosure, the roof disappear,
And we should cease to be sure of what is real or unreal?
Hold tight, hold tight, we must insist that the world is what
    we have always taken it to be.

AMY'S VOICE

Ivy! Violet! has Arthur or John come yet?

IVY

There is no news of Arthur or John.
[*Enter* AMY *and* AGATHA]

AMY

It is very annoying. They both promised to be here
In good time for dinner. It is very annoying.
Now they can hardly arrive in time to dress.
I do not understand what could have gone wrong
With both of them, coming from different directions.
Well, we must go and dress, I suppose. I hope Harry will feel
    better
After his rest upstairs.

[*Exeunt, except* AGATHA]

Scene II

AGATHA

[*Enter* MARY *with flowers*]

MARY

The spring is very late in this northern country,
Late and uncertain, clings to the south wall.
The gardener had no garden-flowers to give me for this
    evening.

AGATHA

I always forget how late the spring is, here.

MARY

I had rather wait for our windblown blossoms,
Such as they are, than have these greenhouse flowers
Which do not belong here, which do not know
The wind and rain, as I know them.

AGATHA

I wonder how many we shall be for dinner.

MARY

Seven . . . nine . . . ten surely.

I hear that Harry has arrived already
And he was the only one that was uncertain.
Arthur or John may be late, of course.
We may have to keep the dinner back . . .

AGATHA

And also Dr. Warburton. At least, Amy has invited him.

MARY

Dr. Warburton? I think she might have told me;
It is very difficult, having to plan
For uncertain numbers. Why did she ask him?

AGATHA

She only thought of asking him a little while ago.

MARY

Well, there's something to be said for having an outsider;
For what is more formal than a family dinner?
An official occasion of uncomfortable people
Who meet very seldom, making conversation.
I am very glad if Dr. Warburton is coming.
I shall have to sit between Arthur and John.
Which is worse, thinking of what to say to John,
Or having to listen to Arthur's chatter
When he thinks he is behaving like a man of the world?
Cousin Agatha, I want your advice.

AGATHA

                         I should have thought
You had more than you wanted of that, when at college.

I might have known you'd throw that up against me.
I know I wasn't one of your favourite students:
I only saw you as a hard headmistress
Who knew the way of dominating timid girls.
I don't see you any differently now;
But I really wish that I'd taken your advice
And tried for a fellowship, seven years ago.
Now I want your advice, because there's no one else to ask,
And because you are strong, and because you don't belong
    here
Any more than I do. I want to get away.

AGATHA

After seven years?

MARY

Oh, you don't understand!
But you do understand. You only want to know
Whether I understand. You know perfectly well,
What Cousin Amy wants, she usually gets.
Why do *you* so seldom come here? *You*'re not afraid of her,
But I think you must have wanted to avoid collision.
I suppose I could have gone, if I'd had the moral courage,
Even against a will like hers. I know very well
Why she wanted to keep me. She didn't need me:
She would have done just as well with a hired servant
Or with none. She only wanted me for Harry —
Not such a compliment: she only wanted
To have a tame daughter-in-law with very little money,
A housekeeper-companion for her and Harry.
Even when he married, she still held on to me

Because she couldn't bear to let any project go;
And even when *she* died: I believed that Cousin Amy —
I almost believed it — had killed her by willing.
Doesn't that sound awful? I know that it does.
Did you ever meet her? What was she like?

AGATHA

I am the only one who ever met her,
The only one Harry asked to his wedding:
Amy did not know that. I was sorry for her;
I could see that she distrusted me — she was frightened of
    the family,
She wanted to fight them — with the weapons of the weak,
Which are too violent. And it could not have been easy,
Living with Harry. It's not what she did to Harry,
That's important, I think, but what he did to himself.

MARY

But it wasn't till I knew that Harry had returned
That I felt the strength to go. I know I must go.
But where? I want a job: and you can help me.

AGATHA

I am very sorry, Mary, I am very sorry for you;
Though you may not think me capable of such a feeling.
I would like to help you: but you must not run away.
Any time before now, it would have shown courage
And would have been right. Now, the courage is only the
    moment
And the moment is only fear and pride. I see more than this,
More than I can tell you, more than there are words for.
At this moment, there is no decision to be made;

46

The decision will be made by powers beyond us
Which now and then emerge. You and I, Mary,
Are only watchers and waiters: not the easiest rôle.
I must go and change for dinner.

[*Exit*]

MARY

So you will not help me!
Waiting, waiting, always waiting.
I think this house *means* to keep us waiting.
[*Enter* HARRY]

HARRY

Waiting? For what?

MARY

How do you do, Harry.
You are down very early. I thought you had just arrived.
Did you have a comfortable journey?

HARRY

Not very.
But, at least, it did not last long. How are you, Mary?

MARY

Oh, very well. What are you looking for?

HARRY

I had only just noticed that this room is quite unchanged:
The same hangings . . . the same pictures . . . even the table,
The chairs, the sofa . . . all in the same positions.
I was looking to see if anything was changed,
But if so, I can't find it.

MARY

Your mother insisted
On everything being kept the same as when you left it.

HARRY

I wish she had not done that. It's very unnatural,
This arresting of the normal change of things:
But it's very like her. What I might have expected.
It only makes the changing of people
All the more manifest.

MARY

Yes, nothing changes here,
And we just go on . . . drying up, I suppose,
Not noticing the change. But to you, I am sure,
We must seem very altered.

HARRY

You have hardly changed at all —
And I haven't seen you since you came down from Oxford.

MARY

Well, I must go and change for dinner.
We do change — to that extent.

HARRY

No, don't go just yet.

MARY

Are you glad to be at home?

HARRY

There was something

I wanted to ask you. I don't know yet.
All these years I'd been longing to get back
Because I thought I never should. I thought it was a place
Where life was substantial and simplified —
But the simplification took place in my memory,
I think. It seems I shall get rid of nothing,
Of none of the shadows that I wanted to escape;
And at the same time, other memories,
Earlier, forgotten, begin to return
Out of my childhood. I can't explain.
But I thought I might escape from one life to another,
And it may be all one life, with no escape. Tell me,
Were you ever happy here, as a child at Wishwood?

MARY

Happy? not really, though I never knew why:
It always seemed that it must be my own fault,
And never to be happy was always to be naughty.
But there were reasons: I was only a cousin
Kept here because there was nothing else to do with me.
I didn't belong here. It was different for you.
And you seemed so much older. We were rather in awe of
        you —
At least, I was.

HARRY

Why were we not happy?

MARY

Well, it all seemed to be imposed upon us;
Even the nice things were laid out ready,
And the treats were always so carefully prepared;

There was never any time to invent our own enjoyments.
But perhaps it was all designed for you, not for us.

HARRY

No, it didn't seem like that. I was part of the design
As well as you. But what was the design?
It never came off. But do you remember

MARY

The hollow tree in what we called the wilderness

HARRY

Down near the river. That was the stockade
From which we fought the Indians, Arthur and John.

MARY

It was the cave where we met by moonlight
To raise the evil spirits.

HARRY

Arthur and John.
Of course we were punished for being out at night
After being put to bed. But at least they never knew
Where we had been.

MARY

They never found the secret.

HARRY

Not then. But later, coming back from school
For the holidays, after the formal reception
And the family festivities, I made my escape

50

As soon as I could, and slipped down to the river
To find the old hiding place. The wilderness was gone,
The tree had been felled, and a neat summer-house
Had been erected, 'to please the children'.
It's absurd that one's only memory of freedom
Should be a hollow tree in a wood by the river.

MARY

But when I was a child I took everything for granted,
Including the stupidity of older people —
They lived in another world, which did not touch me.
Just now, I find them very difficult to bear.
They are always assured that you ought to be happy
At the very moment when you are wholly conscious
Of being a misfit, of being superfluous.
But why should I talk about my commonplace troubles?
They must seem very trivial indeed to you.
It's just ordinary hopelessness.

HARRY

                    One thing you cannot know:
The sudden extinction of every alternative,
The unexpected crash of the iron cataract.
You do not know what hope is, until you have lost it.
You only know what it is not to hope:
You do not know what it is to have hope taken from you,
Or to fling it away, to join the legion of the hopeless
Unrecognised by other men, though sometimes by each
    other.

MARY

I know what you mean. That is an experience

I have not had. Nevertheless, however real,
However cruel, it may be a deception.

HARRY

What I see
May be one dream or another; if there is nothing else
The most real is what I fear. The bright colour fades
Together with the unrecapturable emotion,
The glow upon the world, that never found its object;
And the eye adjusts itself to a twilight
Where the dead stone is seen to be batrachian,
The aphyllous branch ophidian.

MARY

You bring your own landscape
No more real than the other. And in a way you contradict
     yourself:
That sudden comprehension of the death of hope
Of which you speak, I know you have experienced it,
And I can well imagine how awful it must be.
But in this world another hope keeps springing
In an unexpected place, while we are unconscious of it.
You hoped for something, in coming back to Wishwood,
Or you would not have come.

HARRY

Whatever I hoped for
Now that I am here I know I shall not find it.
The instinct to return to the point of departure
And start again as if nothing had happened,
Isn't that all folly? It's like the hollow tree,
Not there.

MARY

But surely, what you say
Only proves that you expected Wishwood
To be your real self, to do something for you
That you can only do for yourself.
What you need to alter is something inside you
Which you can change anywhere — here, as well as else-
    where.

HARRY

Something inside me, you think, that can be altered!
And here, indeed! where I have felt them near me,
Here and here and here — wherever I am not looking,
Always flickering at the corner of my eye,
Almost whispering just out of earshot —
And inside too, in the nightly panic
Of dreaming dissolution. You do not know,
You cannot know, you cannot understand.

MARY

I think I could understand, but you would have to be patient
With me, and with people who have not had your ex-
    perience.

HARRY

If I tried to explain, you could never understand:
Explaining would only make a worse misunderstanding;
Explaining would only set me farther away from you.
There is only one way for you to understand
And that is by seeing. They are much too clever
To admit you into *our* world. Yours is no better.
They have seen to that: it is part of the torment.

MARY

If you think I am incapable of understanding you —
But in any case, I must get ready for dinner.

HARRY

No, no, don't go! Please don't leave me
Just at this moment. I feel it is important.
Something should have come of this conversation.

MARY

I am not a wise person,
And in the ordinary sense I don't know you very well,
Although I remember you better than you think,
And what is the real you. I haven't much experience,
But I see something now which doesn't come from tutors
Or from books, or from thinking, or from observation:
Something which I did not know I knew.
Even if, as you say, Wishwood is a cheat,
Your family a delusion — then it's *all* a delusion,
Everything you feel — I don't mean what you think,
But what you feel. You attach yourself to loathing
As others do to loving: an infatuation
That's wrong, a good that's misdirected. You deceive your-
     self.
Like the man convinced that he is paralysed
Or like the man who believes that he is blind
While he still sees the sunlight. I know that this is true.

HARRY

I have spent many years in useless travel;
You have stayed in England, yet you seem
Like someone who comes from a very long distance,

Or the distant waterfall in the forest,
Inaccessible, half-heard.
And I hear your voice as in the silence
Between two storms, one hears the moderate usual noises
In the grass and leaves, of life persisting,
Which ordinarily pass unnoticed.
Perhaps you are right, though I do not know
How you should know it. Is the cold spring
Is the spring not an evil time, that excites us with lying
    voices?

MARY

The cold spring now is the time
For the ache in the moving root
The agony in the dark
The slow flow throbbing the trunk
The pain of the breaking bud.
These are the ones that suffer least:
The aconite under the snow
And the snowdrop crying for a moment in the wood.

HARRY

Spring is an issue of blood
A season of sacrifice
And the wail of the new full tide
Returning the ghosts of the dead
Those whom the winter drowned
Do not the ghosts of the drowned
Return to land in the spring?
Do the dead want to return?

MARY

Pain is the opposite of joy

But joy is a kind of pain
I believe the moment of birth
Is when we have knowledge of death
I believe the season of birth
Is the season of sacrifice
For the tree and the beast, and the fish
Thrashing itself upstream:
And what of the terrified spirit
Compelled to be reborn
To rise toward the violent sun
Wet wings into the rain cloud
Harefoot over the moon?

HARRY

What have we been saying? I think I was saying
That it seemed as if I had been always here
And you were someone who had come from a long distance.
Whether I know what I am saying, or why I say it,
That does not matter. You bring me news
Of a door that opens at the end of a corridor,
Sunlight and singing; when I had felt sure
That every corridor only led to another,
Or to a blank wall; that I kept moving
Only so as not to stay still. Singing and light.
Stop!
What is that? do you feel it?

MARY
What, Harry?

HARRY
That apprehension deeper than all sense,

56

Deeper than the sense of smell, but like a smell
In that it is indescribable, a sweet and bitter smell
From another world. I know it, I know it!
More potent than ever before, a vapour dissolving
All other worlds, and me into it. O Mary!
Don't look at me like that! Stop! Try to stop it!
I am going. Oh why, now? Come out!
Come out! Where are you? Let me see you,
Since I know you are there, I know you are spying on me.
Why do you play with me, why do you let me go,
Only to surround me? — When I remember them
They leave me alone: when I forget them
Only for an instant of inattention
They are roused again, the sleepless hunters
That will not let me sleep. At the moment before sleep
I always see their claws distended
Quietly, as if they had never stirred.
It was only a moment, it was only one moment
That I stood in sunlight, and thought I might stay there.

MARY

Look at me. You can depend on me.
Harry! Harry! It's all *right*, I tell you.
If you will depend on me, it will be all right.

HARRY

Come out!
[*The curtains part, revealing the Eumenides in the window
        embrasure*]
Why do you show yourselves now for the first time?
When I knew her, I was not the same person.
I was not any person. Nothing that I did

Has to do with me. The accident of a dreaming moment,
Of a dreaming age, when I was someone else
Thinking of something else, puts me among you.
I tell you, it is not me you are looking at,
Not me you are grinning at, not me your confidential looks
Incriminate, but that other person, if person
You thought I was: let your necrophily
Feed upon that carcass. They will not go.

MARY

Harry! There is no one here.
[*She goes to the window and pulls the curtains across*]

HARRY

They were here, I tell you. They are here.
Are you so imperceptive, have you such dull senses
That you could not see them? If I had realised
That you were so obtuse, I would not have listened
To your nonsense. Can't you help me?
You're of no use to me. I must face them.
I must fight them. But they are stupid.
How can one fight with stupidity?
Yet I must speak to them.
[*He rushes forward and tears apart the curtains: but the
embrasure is empty*]

MARY
Oh, Harry!

Scene III

HARRY, MARY, IVY, VIOLET, GERALD, CHARLES

VIOLET

Good evening, Mary: aren't you dressed yet?
How do you think that Harry is looking?
Why, who could have pulled those curtains apart?
[*Pulls them together*]
Very well, I think, after such a long journey;
You know what a rush he had to be here in time
For his mother's birthday.

IVY

Mary, my dear,
Did you arrange these flowers? Just let me change them.
You don't mind, do you? I know so much about flowers;
Flowers have always been my passion.
You know I had my own garden once, in Cornwall,
When I could afford a garden; and I took several prizes
With my delphiniums. I was rather an authority.

GERALD

Good evening, Mary. You've seen Harry, I see.
It's good to have him back again, isn't it?

We must make him feel at home. And most auspicious
That he could be here for his mother's birthday.

MARY

I must go and change. I came in very late.

[*Exit*]

CHARLES

Now we only want Arthur and John
I am glad that you'll all be together, Harry;
They need the influence of their elder brother.
Arthur's a bit irresponsible, you know;
You should have a sobering effect upon him.
After all, you're the head of the family.

AMY'S VOICE

Violet! Has Arthur or John come yet?

VIOLET

Neither of them is here yet, Amy.
[*Enter* AMY, *with* DR. WARBURTON]

AMY

It is most vexing. What can have happened?
I suppose it's the fog that is holding them up,
So it's no use to telephone anywhere. Harry!
Haven't you seen Dr. Warburton?
You know he's the oldest friend of the family,
And he's known you longer than anybody, Harry.
When he heard that you were going to be here for
        dinner
He broke an important engagement to come.

60

WARBURTON

I dare say we've both changed a good deal, Harry.
A country practitioner doesn't get younger.
It takes me back longer than you can remember
To see you again. But you can't have forgotten
The day when you came back from school with measles
And we had such a time to keep you in bed.
You didn't like being ill in the holidays.

IVY

It *was* unpleasant, coming home to have an illness.

VIOLET

It was always the same with your minor ailments
And children's epidemics: you would never stay in bed
Because you were convinced that you would never get well.

HARRY

Not, I think, without some justification:
For what you call restoration to health
Is only incubation of another malady.

WARBURTON

You mustn't take such a pessimistic view
Which is hardly complimentary to my profession.
But I remember, when I was a student at Cambridge,
I used to dream of making some great discovery
To do away with one disease or another.
Now I've had forty years' experience
I've left off thinking in terms of the laboratory.
We're all of us ill in one way or another:
We call it health when we find no symptom
Of illness. Health is a relative term.

IVY

You must have had a very rich experience, Doctor,
In forty years.

WARBURTON
Indeed, yes.
Even in a country practice. My first patient, now —
You wouldn't believe it, ladies — was a murderer,
Who suffered from an incurable cancer.
How he fought against it! I never saw a man
More anxious to live.

HARRY
Not at all extraordinary.
It is really harder to believe in murder
Than to believe in cancer. Cancer is here:
The lump, the dull pain, the occasional sickness:
Murder a reversal of sleep and waking.
Murder was there. Your ordinary murderer
Regards himself as an innocent victim.
To himself he is still what he used to be
Or what he would be. He cannot realise
That everything is irrevocable,
The past unredeemable. But cancer, now,
That is something real.

WARBURTON
Well, let's not talk of such matters.
How did we get on to the subject of cancer?
I really don't know. — But now you're all grown up
I haven't a patient left at Wishwood.
Wishwood was always a cold place, but healthy.

62

It's only when I get an invitation to dinner
That I ever see your mother.

VIOLET
                    Yes, look at your mother!
Except that she can't get about now in winter
You wouldn't think that she was a day older
Than on her birthday ten years ago.

GERALD
Is there any use in waiting for Arthur and John?

AMY
We might as well go in to dinner.
They may come before we finish. Will you take me in,
        Doctor?
I think we are very much the oldest present —
In fact we are the oldest inhabitants.
As we came first, we will go first, in to dinner.

WARBURTON
With pleasure, Lady Monchensey,
And I hope that next year will bring me the same honour.
                    [*Exeunt* AMY, DR. WARBURTON, HARRY]

CHORUS
I am afraid of all that has happened, and of all that is to
        come;
Of the things to come that sit at the door, as if they had been
        there always.
And the past is about to happen, and the future was long
        since settled.

And the wings of the future darken the past, the beak and
    claws have desecrated
History. Shamed
The first cry in the bedroom, the noise in the nursery,
    mutilated
The family album, rendered ludicrous
The tenants' dinner, the family picnic on the moors. Have
    torn
The roof from the house, or perhaps it was never there.
And the bird sits on the broken chimney. I am afraid.

IVY

This is a most undignified terror, and I must struggle
    against it.

GERALD

I am used to tangible danger, but only to what I can under-
    stand.

VIOLET

It is the obtuseness of Gerald and Charles and that doctor,
    that gets on my nerves.

CHARLES

If the matter were left in my hands, I think I could manage
    the situation.

[Exeunt]
[Enter MARY, and passes through to dinner. Enter AGATHA]

AGATHA

The eye is on this house
The eye covers it

There are three together
May the three be separated
May the knot that was tied
Become unknotted
May the crossed bones
In the filled-up well
Be at last straightened
May the weasel and the otter
Be about their proper business
The eye of the day time
And the eye of the night time
Be diverted from this house
Till the knot is unknotted
The crossed is uncrossed
And the crooked is made straight.

[Exit to dinner]

END OF PART I

Part II

The Library, after Dinner

Scene I

WARBURTON

I'm glad of a few minutes alone with you, Harry.
In fact, I had another reason for coming this evening
Than simply in honour of your mother's birthday.
I wanted a private conversation with you
On a confidential matter.

HARRY

I can imagine —
Though I think it is probably going to be useless,
Or if anything, make matters rather more difficult.
But talk about it, if you like.

WARBURTON

You don't understand me.
I'm sure you cannot know what is on my mind;
And as for making matters more difficult —
It is much more difficult not to be prepared
For something that is very likely to happen.

HARRY

O God, man, the things that are going to happen

Have already happened.

WARBURTON
                    That is in a sense true,
But without your knowing it, and what you know
Or do not know, at any moment
May make an endless difference to the future.
It's about your mother . . .

HARRY
                    What about my mother?
Everything has always been referred back to mother.
When we were children, before we went to school,
The rule of conduct was simply pleasing mother;
Misconduct was simply being unkind to mother;
What was wrong was whatever made her suffer,
And whatever made her happy was what was virtuous —
Though never very happy, I remember. That was why
We all felt like failures, before we had begun.
When we came back, for the school holidays,
They were not holidays, but simply a time
In which we were supposed to make up to mother
For all the weeks during which she had not seen us
Except at half-term, and seeing us then
Only seemed to make her more unhappy, and made us
Feel more guilty, and so we misbehaved
Next day at school, in order to be punished,
For punishment made us feel less guilty. Mother
Never punished us, but made us feel guilty.
I think that the things that are taken for granted
At home, make a deeper impression upon children
Than what they are told.

WARBURTON

Stop, Harry, you're mistaken.
I mean, you don't know what I want to tell you.
You may be quite right, but what we are concerned with
Now, is your mother's happiness in the future,
For the time she has to live: not with the past.

HARRY

Oh, is there any difference!
How can we be concerned with the past
And not with the future? or with the future
And not with the past? What I'm telling you
Is very important. Very important.
You must let me explain, and then you can talk.
I don't know why, but just this evening
I feel an overwhelming need for explanation —
But perhaps I only dream that I am talking
And shall wake to find that I have been silent
Or talked to the stone deaf: and the others
Seem to hear something else than what I am saying.
But if you want to talk, at least you can tell me
Something useful. Do you remember my father?

WARBURTON

Why, yes, of course, Harry, but I really don't see
What that has to do with the present occasion
Or with what I have to tell you.

HARRY

What you have to tell me
Is either something that I know already
Or unimportant, or else untrue.

71

But I want to know more about my father.
I hardly remember him, and I know very well
That I was kept apart from him, till he went away.
We never heard him mentioned, but in some way or another
We felt that he was always here.
But when we would have grasped for him, there was only a
    vacuum
Surrounded by whispering aunts: Ivy and Violet —
Agatha never came then. Where was my father?

WARBURTON

Harry, there's no good probing for misery.
There was enough once: but what festered
Then, has only left a cautery.
Leave it alone. You know that your mother
And your father were never very happy together:
They separated by mutual consent
And he went to live abroad. You were only a boy
When he died. You would not remember.

HARRY

But now I do remember. Not Arthur or John,
They were too young. But now I remember
A summer day of unusual heat,
The day I lost my butterfly net;
I remember the silence, and the hushed excitement
And the low conversation of triumphant aunts.
It is the conversations not overheard,
Not intended to be heard, with the sidewise looks,
That bring death into the heart of a child.
That was the day he died. Of course.
I mean, I suppose, the day on which the news arrived.

WARBURTON

You overinterpret.
I am sure that your mother always loved him;
There was never the slightest suspicion of scandal.

HARRY

Scandal? who said scandal? I did not.
Yes, I see now. That night, when she kissed me,
I felt the trap close. If you won't tell me,
I must ask Agatha. I never dared before.

WARBURTON

I advise you strongly, not to ask your aunt —
I mean, there is nothing she could tell you. But, Harry,
We can't sit here all evening, you know;
You will have to have the birthday celebration,
And your brothers will be here. Won't you let me tell you
What I had to say?

HARRY
Very well, tell me.

WARBURTON

It's about your mother's health that I wanted to talk to you.
I must tell you, Harry, that although your mother
Is still so alert, so vigorous of mind,
Although she seems as vital as ever —
It is only the force of her personality,
Her indomitable will, that keeps her alive.
I needn't go into technicalities
At the present moment. The whole machine is weak
And running down. Her heart's very feeble.

With care, and avoiding all excitement
She may live several years. A sudden shock
Might send her off at any moment.
If she had been another woman
She would not have lived until now.
Her determination has kept her going:
She has only lived for your return to Wishwood,
For you to take command at Wishwood,
And for that reason, it is most essential
That nothing should disturb or excite her.

HARRY

Well!

WARBURTON

I'm very sorry for you, Harry.
I should have liked to spare you this,
Just now. But there were two reasons
Why you had to know. One is your mother,
To make her happy for the time she has to live.
The other is yourself: the future of Wishwood
Depends on you. I don't like to say this;
But you know that I am a very old friend,
And have always been a party to the family secrets —
You know as well as I do that Arthur and John
Have been a great disappointment to your mother.
John's very steady — but he's not exactly brilliant;
And Arthur has always been rather irresponsible.
Your mother's hopes are all centred on you.

HARRY

Hopes? . . . Tell me
Did you know my father at about my present age?

74

WARBURTON

Why, yes, Harry, of course I did.

HARRY

What did he look like then? Did he look at all like me?

WARBURTON

Very much like you. Of course there are differences:
But, allowing for the changes in fashion
And your being clean-shaven, very much like you.
And now, Harry, let's talk about yourself.

HARRY

I never saw a photograph. There is no portrait.

WARBURTON

What I want to know is, whether you've been sleeping . . .
[*Enter* DENMAN]

DENMAN

It's Sergeant Winchell is here, my Lord,
And wants to see your Lordship very urgent,
And Dr. Warburton. He says it's very urgent
Or he wouldn't have troubled you.

HARRY

I'll see him.

[*Exit* DENMAN]

WARBURTON

I wonder what he wants. I hope nothing has happened
To either of your brothers.

HARRY

                    Nothing can have happened
To either of my brothers. Nothing can happen —
If Sergeant Winchell is real. But Denman saw him.
But what if Denman saw him, and yet he was not real?
That would be worse than anything that has happened.
What if *you* saw him, and . . .

WARBURTON

                    Harry! Pull yourself together.
Something may have happened to one of your brothers.
[*Enter* WINCHELL]

WINCHELL

Good evening, my Lord. Good evening, Doctor.
Many happy . . . Oh, I'm sorry, my Lord,
I was thinking it was your birthday, not her Ladyship's.

HARRY

Her Ladyship's!
    [*He darts at* WINCHELL *and seizes him by the shoulders*]
                    He *is* real, Doctor.
So let us resume the conversation. You, and I
And Winchell. Sit down, Winchell,
And have a glass of port. We were talking of my father.

WINCHELL

Always at your jokes, I see. You don't look a year older
Than when I saw you last, my Lord. But a country
        sergeant
Doesn't get younger. Thank you, no, my Lord;
I don't find port agrees with the rheumatism.

WARBURTON

For God's sake, Winchell, tell us your business.
His Lordship isn't very well this evening.

WINCHELL

I understand, Sir.
It'd be the same if it was my birthday —
I beg pardon, I'm forgetting.
If it was my mother's. God rest her soul,
She's been dead these ten years. How is her Ladyship,
If I may ask, my Lord?

HARRY

Why do you keep asking
About her Ladyship? Do you know or don't you?
I'm not afraid of you.

WINCHELL

I should hope not, my Lord.
I didn't mean to put myself forward.
But you see, my Lord, I had good reason for asking . . .

HARRY

Well, do you want me to produce her for you?

WINCHELL

Oh no indeed, my Lord, I'd much rather not . . .

HARRY

You mean you think I can't. But I might surprise you;
I think I might be able to give you a shock.

77

WINCHELL

There's been shock enough for one evening, my Lord:
That's what I've come about.

WARBURTON
                    For Heaven's sake, Winchell,
Tell us your business.

WINCHELL
                    It's about Mr. John.

HARRY

John!

WINCHELL
        Yes, my Lord, I'm sorry.
I thought I'd better have a word with you quiet,
Rather than phone and perhaps disturb her Ladyship.
So I slipped along on my bike. Mostly walking,
What with the fog so thick, or I'd have been here sooner.
I'd telephoned to Dr. Warburton's,
And they told me he was here, and that you'd arrived.
Mr. John's had a bit of an accident
On the West Road, in the fog, coming along
At a pretty smart pace, I fancy, ran into a lorry
Drawn up round the bend. We'll have the driver up for
        this:
Says he doesn't know this part of the country
And stopped to take his bearings. We've got him at the
        Arms —
Mr. John, I mean. By a bit of luck
Dr. Owen was there, and looked him over;

78

Says there's nothing wrong but some nasty cuts
And a bad concussion; says he'll come round
In the morning, most likely, but he mustn't be moved.
But Dr. Owen was anxious that you should have a look at
    him.

WARBURTON
Quite right, quite right. I'll go and have a look at him.
We must explain to your mother . . .

AMY'S VOICE
                  Harry! Harry!
Who's there with you? Is it Arthur or John?
[*Enter* AMY, *followed severally by* VIOLET, IVY, AGATHA,
    GERALD *and* CHARLES]
Winchell! what are you here for?

WINCHELL
I'm sorry, my Lady, but I've just told the doctor,
It's really nothing but a minor accident.

WARBURTON
It's John has had the accident, Lady Monchensey;
And Winchell tells me Dr. Owen has seen him
And says it's nothing but a slight concussion,
But he mustn't be moved tonight. I'd trust Owen
On a matter like this. You can trust Owen.
We'll bring him up tomorrow; and a few days' rest,
I've no doubt, will be all that he needs.

AMY
Accident? What sort of an accident?

79

WINCHELL

Coming along in the fog, my Lady,
And he must have been in rather a hurry.
There was a lorry drawn up where it shouldn't be,
Outside of the village, on the West Road.

AMY

Where is he?

WINCHELL

At the Arms, my Lady;
Of course, he hasn't come round yet.
Dr. Owen was there, by a bit of luck.

GERALD

I'll go down and see him, Amy, and come back and report
to you.

AMY

I must see for myself. Order the car at once.

WARBURTON

I forbid it, Lady Monchensey.
As your doctor, I forbid you to leave the house tonight.
There is nothing you could do, and out in this weather
At this time of night, I would not answer for the conse-
quences.
I am going myself. I will come back and report to you.

AMY

I must see for myself. I do not believe you.

CHARLES

Much better leave it to Warburton, Amy.

Extremely fortunate for us that he's here.
We must put ourselves under Warburton's orders.

WARBURTON

I repeat, Lady Monchensey, that you must not go out.
If you do, I must decline to continue to treat you.
You are only delaying me. I shall return at once.

AMY

Well, I suppose you are right. But can I trust you?

WARBURTON

You have trusted me a good many years, Lady Monchensey;
This is not the time to begin to doubt me.
Come, Winchell. We can put your bicycle
On the back of my car.

[*Exeunt* WARBURTON *and* WINCHELL]

VIOLET

Well, Harry,
I think that you might have had something to say.
Aren't you sorry for your brother? Aren't you aware
Of what is going on? and what it means to your mother?

HARRY

Oh, of course I'm sorry. But from what Winchell says
I don't think the matter can be very serious.
A minor trouble like a concussion
Cannot make very much difference to John.
A brief vacation from the kind of consciousness
That John enjoys, can't make very much difference
To him or to anyone else. If he was ever really conscious,

81

I should be glad for him to have a breathing spell:
But John's ordinary day isn't much more than breathing.

IVY

Really, Harry! how can you be so callous?
I always thought you were so fond of John.

VIOLET

And if you don't care what happens to John,
You might show some consideration to your mother.

AMY

I do not know very much:
And as I get older, I am coming to think
How little I have ever known.
But I think your remarks are much more inappropriate
Than Harry's.

HARRY

It's only when they see nothing
That people can always show the suitable emotions —
And so far as they feel at all, their emotions are suitable.
They don't understand what it is to be awake,
To be living on several planes at once
Though one cannot speak with several voices at once.
I have all of the rightminded feeling about John
That you consider appropriate. Only, that's not the language
That I choose to be talking. I will not talk yours.

AMY

You looked like your father
When you said that.

HARRY

I think, mother,
I shall make you lie down. You must be very tired.

[*Exeunt* HARRY *and* AMY]

VIOLET

I really do not understand Harry's behaviour.

AGATHA

I think it is as well to leave Harry to establish
If he can, some communication with his mother.

VIOLET

I do not seem to be very popular tonight.

CHARLES

Well, there's no sort of use in any of us going —
On a night like this — it's a good three miles;
There's nothing we could do that Warburton can't.
If he's worse than Winchell said, then he'll let us know at
    once.

GERALD

I am really more afraid of the shock for Amy;
But I think that Warburton understands *that*.

IVY

You are quite right, Gerald, the one thing that matters
Is not to let her see that anyone is worried.
We must carry on as if nothing had happened,
And have the cake and presents.

GERALD

But *I*'m worried about Arthur:
He's much more apt than John to get into trouble.

CHARLES

Oh, but Arthur's a brilliant driver.
After all the experience he's had at Brooklands,
He's not likely to get into trouble.

GERALD

A brilliant driver, but more reckless.

IVY

Yet I remember, when they were boys,
Arthur was always the more adventurous
But John was the one that had the accidents,
Somehow, just because he *was* the slow one.
He was always the one to fall off the pony,
Or out of a tree — and always on his head.

VIOLET

But a year ago, Arthur took me out in his car,
And I told him I would never go out with him again.
Not that I wanted to go with him at all —
Though of course he meant well — but I think an open car
Is so undignified: you're blown about so,
And you feel so conspicuous, lolling back
And so near the street, and everyone staring;
And the pace he went at was simply terrifying.
I said I would rather walk: and I did.

GERALD

Walk? where to?

VIOLET

He started out to take me to Cheltenham;
But I stopped him somewhere in Chiswick, I think.
Anyway, the district was unfamiliar
And I had the greatest trouble in getting home.
I am sure he meant well. But I do think he is reckless.

GERALD

I wonder how much Amy knows about Arthur?

CHARLES

More than she cares to mention, I imagine.
[*Enter* HARRY]

HARRY

Mother is asleep, I think: it's strange how the old
Can drop off to sleep in the middle of calamity
Like children, or like hardened campaigners. She looked
Very much as she must have looked when she was a child.
You've been holding a meeting — the usual family inquest
On the characters of all the junior members?
Or engaged in predicting the minor event,
Engaged in foreseeing the minor disaster?
You go on trying to think of each thing separately,
Making small things important, so that everything
May be unimportant, a slight deviation
From some imaginary course that life ought to take,
That you call normal. What you call the normal
Is merely the unreal and the unimportant.
I was like that in a way, so long as I could think
Even of my own life as an isolated ruin,
A casual bit of waste in an orderly universe.

85

But it begins to seem just part of some huge disaster,
Some monstrous mistake and aberration
Of all men, of the world, which I cannot put in order.
If you only knew the years that I have had to live
Since I came home, a few hours ago, to Wishwood.

VIOLET

I will make no observation on what you say, Harry;
My comments are not always welcome in this family.
[*Enter* DENMAN]

DENMAN

Excuse me, Miss Ivy. There's a trunk call for you.

IVY

A trunk call? for me? why who can want me?

DENMAN

He wouldn't give his name, Miss; but it's Mr. Arthur.

IVY

Arthur! Oh dear, I'm afraid *he's* had an accident.
[*Exeunt* IVY *and* DENMAN]

VIOLET

When it's Ivy that he's asking for, I expect the worst.

AGATHA

Whatever you have learned, Harry, you must remember
That there is always more: we cannot rest in being
The impatient spectators of malice or stupidity.
We must try to penetrate the other private worlds

Of make-believe and fear. To rest in our own suffering
Is evasion of suffering. We must learn to suffer more.

VIOLET

Agatha's remarks are invariably pointed.

HARRY

Do you think that I believe what I said just now?
That was only what I should like to believe.
I was talking in abstractions: and you answered in ab-
    stractions.
I have a private puzzle. Were they simply outside,
I might escape somewhere, perhaps. Were they simply
    inside
I could cheat them perhaps with the aid of Dr. Warburton—
Or any other doctor, who would be another Warburton,
If you decided to set another doctor on me.
But this is too real for your words to alter.
Oh, there *must* be another way of talking
That would get us somewhere. You don't understand me.
You can't understand me. It's not being alone
That is the horror — to be alone with the horror.
What matters is the filthiness. I can clean my skin,
Purify my life, void my mind,
But always the filthiness, that lies a little deeper . . .
[*Enter* IVY]

IVY

Where is there an evening paper?

GERALD
                        Why, what's the matter?

87

IVY

Somebody, look for Arthur in the evening paper.
That was Arthur, ringing up from London:
The connection was so bad, I could hardly hear him,
And his voice was very queer. It seems that Arthur too
Has had an accident. I don't think he's hurt,
But he says that he hasn't got the use of his car,
And he missed the last train, so he's coming up tomorrow;
And he said there was something about it in the paper,
But it's all a mistake. And not to tell his mother.

VIOLET

What's the use of asking for an evening paper?
You know as well as I do, at this distance from London
Nobody's likely to have this evening's paper.

CHARLES

Stop, I think I bought a lunch edition
Before I left St. Pancras. If I did, it's in my overcoat.
I'll see if it's there. There might be something in that.

[Exit]

GERALD

Well, I said that Arthur was every bit as likely
To have an accident as John. And it wasn't John's fault,
I don't believe. John is unlucky,
But Arthur is definitely reckless.

VIOLET

I think these racing cars ought to be prohibited.
[Re-enter CHARLES, with a newspaper]

CHARLES

Yes, there is a paragraph . . . I'm glad to say
It's not very conspicuous . . .

GERALD

There'll have been more in the later editions.
You'd better read it to us.

CHARLES [*reads*]
'*Peer's Brother in Motor Smash*'

'The Hon. Arthur Gerald Charles Piper, younger brother of
Lord Monchensey, who ran into and demolished a
roundsman's cart in Ebury Street early on the morning
of January 1st, was fined £50 and costs to-day, and
forbidden to drive a car for the next twelve months.

'While trying to extricate his car from the collision, Mr.
Piper reversed into a shop-window. When challenged,
Mr. Piper said: "I thought it was all open country about
here" —'

GERALD

Where?

CHARLES

In Ebury Street. 'The police stated that at the time of the
accident Mr. Piper was being pursued by a patrol, and was
travelling at the rate of 66 miles an hour. When asked
why he did not stop when signalled by the police car,
he said: "I thought you were having a game with
me." '

GERALD

This is what the Communists make capital out of.

89

CHARLES

There's a little more. 'The Piper family . . .' no, we needn't
    read that.

VIOLET

This is just what I expected. But if Agatha
Is going to moralise about it, I shall scream.

GERALD

It's going to be awkward, explaining this to Amy.

IVY

Poor Arthur! I'm sure that you're being much too hard on
    him.

CHARLES

In my time, these affairs were kept out of the papers;
But nowadays, there's no such thing as privacy.

CHORUS

In an old house there is always listening, and more is heard
    than is spoken.
And what is spoken remains in the room, waiting for the
    future to hear it.
And whatever happens began in the past, and presses hard
    on the future.
The agony in the curtained bedroom, whether of birth or of
    dying,
Gathers into itself all the voices of the past, and projects
    them into the future.
The treble voices on the lawn
The mowing of hay in summer

The dogs and the old pony
The stumble and the wail of little pain
The chopping of wood in autumn
And the singing in the kitchen
And the steps at night in the corridor
The moment of sudden loathing
And the season of stifled sorrow
The whisper, the transparent deception
The keeping up of appearances
The making the best of a bad job
All twined and tangled together, all are recorded.
There is no avoiding these things
And we know nothing of exorcism
And whether in Argos or England
There are certain inflexible laws
Unalterable, in the nature of music.
There is nothing at all to be done about it,
There is nothing to do about anything,
And now it is nearly time for the news
We must listen to the weather report
And the international catastrophes.

[*Exeunt* CHORUS]

Scene II

Harry

John will recover, be what he always was;
Arthur again be sober, though not for very long;
And everything will go on as before. These mild surprises
Should be in the routine of normal life at Wishwood.
John is the only one of us I can conceive
As settling down to make himself at home at Wishwood,
Make a dull marriage, marry some woman stupider —
Stupider than himself. He can resist the influence
Of Wishwood, being unconscious, living in gentle motion
Of horses, and right visits to the right neighbours
At the right times; and be an excellent landlord.

Agatha

What is in your mind, Harry?
I can guess about the past and what you mean about the
    future;
But a present is missing, needed to connect them.
You may be afraid that I would not understand you,
You may also be afraid of being understood,
Try not to regard it as an explanation.

I still have to learn exactly what their meaning is.
At the beginning, eight years ago,
I felt, at first, that sense of separation,
Of isolation unredeemable, irrevocable —
It's eternal, or gives a knowledge of eternity,
Because it feels eternal while it lasts. That is one hell.
Then the numbness came to cover it — that is another —
That was the second hell of not being there,
The degradation of being parted from myself,
From the self which persisted only as an eye, seeing.
All this last year, I could not fit myself together:
When I was inside the old dream, I felt all the same
          emotion
Or lack of emotion, as before: the same loathing
Diffused, I not a person, in a world not of persons
But only of contaminating presences.
And then I had no horror of my action,
I only felt the repetition of it
Over and over. When I was outside,
I could associate nothing of it with myself,
Though nothing else was real. I thought foolishly
That when I got back to Wishwood, as I had left it,
Everything would fall into place. But *they* prevent it.
I still have to find out what their meaning is.
Here I have been finding
A misery long forgotten, and a new torture,
The shadow of something behind our meagre child-
          hood,
Some origin of wretchedness. Is that what they would show
          me?
And now I want you to tell me about my father.

AGATHA

What do you want to know about your father?

HARRY

If I knew, then I should not have to ask.
You know what I want to know, and that is enough:
Warburton told me that, though he did not mean to.
What I want to know is something I need to know,
And only you can tell me. I know that much.

AGATHA

I had to fight for many years to win my dispossession,
And many years to keep it. What people know me as,
The efficient principal of a women's college —
That is the surface. There is a deeper
Organisation, which your question disturbs.

HARRY

When I know, I know that in some way I shall find
That I have always known it. And that will be better.

AGATHA

I will try to tell you. I hope I have the strength.

HARRY

I have thought of you as the completely strong,
The liberated from the human wheel.
So I looked to you for strength. Now I think it is
A common pursuit of liberation.

AGATHA

Your father might have lived — or so I see him —
An exceptionally cultivated country squire,
Reading, sketching, playing on the flute,

Something of an oddity to his county neighbours,
But not neglecting public duties.
He hid his strength beneath unusual weakness,
The diffidence of a solitary man:
Where he was weak he recognised your mother's power,
And yielded to it.

HARRY

There was no ecstasy.
Tell me now, who were my parents?

AGATHA

Your father and your mother.

HARRY

You tell me nothing.

AGATHA

The dead man whom you have assumed to be your father,
And my sister whom you acknowledge as your mother:
There is no mystery here.

HARRY

What then?

AGATHA

You see your mother as identified with this house —
It was not always so. There were many years
Before she succeeded in making terms with Wishwood,
Until she took your father's place, and reached the point
     where
Wishwood supported her, and she supported Wishwood.
At first it was a vacancy. A man and a woman
Married, alone in a lonely country house together,
For three years childless, learning the meaning

Of loneliness. Your mother wanted a sister here
Always. I was the youngest: I was then
An undergraduate at Oxford. I came
Once for a long vacation. I remember
A summer day of unusual heat
For this cold country.

HARRY
And then?

AGATHA

There are hours when there seems to be no past or future,
Only a present moment of pointed light
When you want to burn. When you stretch out your hand
To the flames. They only come once,
Thank God, that kind. Perhaps there is another kind,
I believe, across a whole Thibet of broken stones
That lie, fang up, a lifetime's march. I have believed this.

HARRY

I have known neither.

AGATHA

The autumn came too soon, not soon enough.
The rain and wind had not shaken your father
Awake yet. I found him thinking
How to get rid of your mother. What simple plots!
He was not suited to the role of murderer.

HARRY

In what way did he wish to murder her?

AGATHA

Oh, a dozen foolish ways, each one abandoned

96

For something more ingenious. You were due in three
      months' time;
You would not have been born in that event: I stopped him.
I can take no credit for a little common sense,
He would have bungled it.

                      I did not want to kill *you*!
You to be killed! What were you then? only a thing called
      'life' —
Something that should have been *mine*, as I felt then.
Most people would not have felt that compunction
If they felt no other. But I wanted you!
If that had happened, I knew I should have carried
Death in life, death through lifetime, death in my womb.
I felt that you were in some way mine!
And that in any case I should have no other child.

HARRY

And have me. That is the way things happen.
Everything is true in a different sense,
A sense that would have seemed meaningless before.
Everything tends towards reconciliation
As the stone falls, as the tree falls. And in the end
That is the completion which at the beginning
Would have seemed the ruin.
Perhaps my life has only been a dream
Dreamt through me by the minds of others. Perhaps
I only dreamt I pushed her.

AGATHA

                So I had supposed. What of it?
What we have written is not a story of detection,
Of crime and punishment, but of sin and expiation.

It is possible that you have not known what sin
You shall expiate, or whose, or why. It is certain
That the knowledge of it must precede the expiation.
It is possible that sin may strain and struggle
In its dark instinctive birth, to come to consciousness
And so find expurgation. It is possible
You are the consciousness of your unhappy family,
Its bird sent flying through the purgatorial flame.
Indeed it is possible. You may learn hereafter,
Moving alone through flames of ice, chosen
To resolve the enchantment under which we suffer.

HARRY

Look, I do not know why,
I feel happy for a moment, as if I had come home.
It is quite irrational, but now
I feel quite happy, as if happiness
Did not consist in getting what one wanted
Or in getting rid of what can't be got rid of
But in a different vision. This is like an end.

AGATHA

And a beginning. Harry, my dear,
I feel very tired, as only the old feel.
The young feel tired at the end of an action —
The old, at the beginning. It is as if
I had been living all these years upon my capital,
Instead of earning my spiritual income daily:
And I am old, to start again to make my living.

HARRY

But you are not unhappy, just now?

98

AGATHA

What does the word mean?
There's relief from a burden that I carried,
And exhaustion at the moment of relief.
The burden's yours now, yours
The burden of all the family. And I am a little frightened.

HARRY

You, frightened! I can hardly imagine it.
I wish I had known — but that was impossible.
I only now begin to have some understanding
Of you, and of all of us. Family affection
Was a kind of formal obligation, a duty
Only noticed by its neglect. One had that part to play.
After such training, I could endure, these ten years,
Playing a part that had been imposed upon me;
And I returned to find another one made ready —
The book laid out, lines underscored, and the costume
Ready to be put on. But it is very odd:
When other people seemed so strong, their apparent
        strength
Stifled my decision. Now I see
I might even become fonder of my mother —
More compassionate at least — by understanding.
But she would not like that. Now I see
I have been wounded in a war of phantoms,
Not by human beings — they have no more power than I.
The things I thought were real are shadows, and the real
Are what I thought were private shadows. O that awful
        privacy
Of the insane mind! Now I can live in public.
Liberty is a different kind of pain from prison.

AGATHA

I only looked through the little door
When the sun was shining on the rose-garden:
And heard in the distance tiny voices
And then a black raven flew over.
And then I was only my own feet walking
Away, down a concrete corridor
In a dead air. Only feet walking
And sharp heel scraping. Over and under
Echo and noise of feet.
I was only the feet, and the eye
Seeing the feet: the unwinking eye
Fixing the movement. Over and under.

HARRY

In and out, in an endless drift
Of shrieking forms in a circular desert
Weaving with contagion of putrescent embraces
On dissolving bone. In and out, the movement
Until the chain broke, and I was left
Under the single eye above the desert.

AGATHA

Up and down, through the stone passages
Of an immense and empty hospital
Pervaded by a smell of disinfectant,
Looking straight ahead, passing barred windows.
Up and down. Until the chain breaks.

HARRY

To and fro, dragging my feet
Among inner shadows in the smoky wilderness,

Trying to avoid the clasping branches
And the giant lizard. To and fro.
Until the chain breaks.

                    The chain breaks,
The wheel stops, and the noise of machinery,
And the desert is cleared, under the judicial sun
Of the final eye, and the awful evacuation
Cleanses.

          I was not there, you were not there, only our
     phantasms
And what did not happen is as true as what did happen
O my dear, and you walked through the little door
And I ran to meet you in the rose-garden.

AGATHA

This is the next moment. This is the beginning.
We do not pass twice through the same door
Or return to the door through which we did not pass.
I have seen the first stage: relief from what happened
Is also relief from that unfulfilled craving
Flattered in sleep, and deceived in waking.

                         You have a long journey.

HARRY

Not yet! not yet! this is the first time that I have been free
From the ring of ghosts with joined hands, from the
     pursuers,
And come into a quiet place.

                    Why is it so quiet?
Do you feel a kind of stirring underneath the air?
Do you? don't you? a communication, a scent
Direct to the brain . . . but not just as before,

Not quite like, not the same . . .

[*The* EUMENIDES *appear*]

and this time

You cannot think that I am surprised to see you.
And you shall not think that I am afraid to see you.
This time, you are real, this time, you are outside me,
And just endurable. I know that you are ready,
Ready to leave Wishwood, and I am going with you.
You followed me here, where I thought I should escape
    you —
No! you were already here before I arrived.
Now I see at last that I am following you,
And I know that there can be only one itinerary
And one destination. Let us lose no time. I will follow.

[*The curtains close.* AGATHA *goes to the window, in a som-
    nambular fashion, and opens the curtains, disclosing the
    empty embrasure. She steps into the place which the*
    EUMENIDES *had occupied.*]

AGATHA

A curse comes to being
As a child is formed.
In both, the incredible
Becomes the actual
Without our intention
Knowing what is intended.
A curse is like a child, formed
In a moment of unconsciousness
In an accidental bed
Or under an elder tree
According to the phase
Of the determined moon.

102

A curse is like a child, formed
To grow to maturity:
Accident is design
And design is accident
In a cloud of unknowing.
O my child, my curse,
You shall be fulfilled:
The knot shall be unknotted
And the crooked made straight.

[*She moves back into the room*]

What have I been saying? I think I was saying
That you have a long journey. You have nothing to stay
     for.
Think of it as like a children's treasure hunt:
Here you have found a clue, hidden in the obvious place.
Delay, and it is lost. Love compels cruelty
To those who do not understand love.
What you have wished to know, what you have learned
Mean the end of a relation, make it impossible.
You did not intend this, I did not intend it,
No one intended, but . . . You must go.

HARRY

Shall we ever meet again?

AGATHA

        Shall we ever meet again?
And who will meet again? Meeting is for strangers.
Meeting is for those who do not know each other.

HARRY

I know that I have made a decision

103

In a moment of clarity, and now I feel dull again.
I only know that I made a decision
Which your words echo. I am still befouled,
But I know there is only one way out of defilement —
Which leads in the end to reconciliation.
And I know that I must go.

AGATHA
You must go.

[*Enter* AMY]

AMY
What are you saying to Harry? He has only arrived,
And you tell him to go?

AGATHA
He shall go.

AMY
He shall go? and who are you to say he shall go?
I think I know well enough why you wish him to go.

AGATHA
I wish nothing. I only say what I know must happen.

AMY
You only say what you intended to happen.

HARRY
Oh, mother,
This is not to do with Agatha, any more than with the rest
of you.

My advice has come from quite a different quarter,
But I cannot explain that to you now. Only be sure
That I know what I am doing, and what I must do,
And that it is the best thing for everybody.
But at present, I cannot explain it to anyone:
I do not know the words in which to explain it —
That is what makes it harder. You must just believe me,
Until I come again.

AMY

But why are you going?

HARRY

              I can only speak
And you cannot hear me. I can only speak
So you may not think I conceal an explanation,
And to tell you that I would have liked to explain.

AMY

Why should Agatha know, and I not be allowed to?

HARRY

I do not know whether Agatha knows
Or how much she knows. Any knowledge she may have —
It was not I who told her . . . All this year,
This last year, I have been in flight
But always in ignorance of invisible pursuers.
Now I know that all my life has been a flight
And phantoms fed upon me while I fled. Now I know
That the last apparent refuge, the safe shelter,
That is where one meets them. That is the way of
      spectres . . .

AMY

There is no one here!
No one, but your family!

HARRY

And now I know
That my business is not to run away, but to pursue,
Not to avoid being found, but to seek.
I would not have chosen this way, had there been any other!
It is at once the hardest thing, and the only thing possible.
Now they will lead me. I shall be safe with them;
I am not safe here.

AMY

So you *will* run away.

AGATHA

In a world of fugitives
The person taking the opposite direction
Will appear to run away.

AMY

I was speaking to Harry.

HARRY

It is very hard, when one has just recovered sanity,
And not yet assured in possession, that is when
One begins to seem the maddest to other people.
It is hard for you too, mother, it is indeed harder,
Not to understand.

AMY

Where are you going?

106

I shall have to learn. That is still unsettled.
I have not yet had the precise directions.
Where does one go from a world of insanity?
Somewhere on the other side of despair.
To the worship in the desert, the thirst and deprivation,
A stony sanctuary and a primitive altar,
The heat of the sun and the icy vigil,
A care over lives of humble people,
The lesson of ignorance, of incurable diseases.
Such things are possible. It is love and terror
Of what waits and wants me, and will not let me fall.
Let the cricket chirp. John shall be the master.
All I have is his. No harm can come to him.
What would destroy me will be life for John,
I am responsible for him. Why I have this election
I do not understand. It must have been preparing always,
And I see it was what I always wanted. Strength demanded
That seems too much, is just strength enough given.
I must follow the bright angels.

                                                    [*Exit*]

Scene III

Amy

I was a fool, to ask you again to Wishwood;
But I thought, thirty-five years is long, and death is an end,
And I thought that time might have made a change in
     Agatha —
It has made enough in *me*. Thirty-five years ago
You took my husband from me. Now you take my son.

Agatha

What did I take? nothing that you ever had.
What did I get? thirty years of solitude,
Alone, among women, in a women's college,
Trying not to dislike women. Thirty years in which to think.
Do you suppose that I wanted to return to Wishwood?

Amy

The more rapacious, to take what I never had;
The more unpardonable, to taunt me with not having it.
Had you taken what I had, you would have left me at least
     a memory
Of something to live upon. You knew that you took everything

108

Except the walls, the furniture, the acres;
Leaving nothing — but what I could breed for myself,
What I could plant here. Seven years I kept him,
For the sake of the future, a discontented ghost,
In his own house. What of the humiliation,
Of the chilly pretences in the silent bedroom,
Forcing sons upon an unwilling father?
Dare you think what that does to one? Try to think of it.
I *would* have sons, if I could not have a husband:
Then I let him go. I abased myself.
Did I show any weakness, any self-pity?
I forced myself to the purposes of Wishwood;
I even asked you back, for visits, after he was gone,
So that there might be no ugly rumours.
You thought I did not know!
You may be close, but I always saw through *him*.
And now it is my son.

AGATHA
              I know one thing, Amy:
That you have never changed. And perhaps I have not.
I thought that I had, until this evening.
But at least I wanted to. Now I must begin.
There is nothing more difficult. But you are just the same:
Just as voracious for what you cannot have
Because you repel it.

AMY
              I prepared the situation
For us to be reconciled, because of Harry,
Because of his mistakes, because of his unhappiness,
Because of the misery that he has left behind him,

Because of the waste. I wanted to obliterate
His past life, and have nothing except to remind him
Of the years when he had been a happy boy at Wishwood;
For his future success.

AGATHA
Success is relative:
It is what we can make of the mess we have made of things,
It is what he can make, not what you would make for him.

AMY
Success is one thing, what you would make for him
Is another. I call it failure. Your fury for possession
Is only the stronger for all these years of abstinence.
Thirty-five years ago you took my husband from me
And now you take my son.

AGATHA
Why should we quarrel for what neither can have?
If neither has ever had a husband or a son
We have no ground for argument.

AMY
Who set you up to judge? what, if you please,
Gives *you* the power to know what is best for Harry?
What gave you this influence to persuade him
To abandon his duty, his family and his happiness?
Who has planned his good? is it you or I?
Thirty-five years designing his life,
Eight years watching, without him, at Wishwood,
Years of bitterness and disappointment.
What share had you in this? what have you given?

110

And now at the moment of success against failure,
When I felt assured of his settlement and happiness,
You who took my husband, now you take my son.
You take him from Wishwood, you take him from me,
You take him . . .
[*Enter* MARY]

MARY

Excuse me, Cousin Amy. I have just seen Denman.
She came to tell me that Harry is leaving:
Downing told her. He has got the car out.
What is the matter?

AMY

That woman there,
She has persuaded him: I do not know how.
I have been always trying to make myself believe
That he was not such a weakling as his father
In the hands of any unscrupulous woman.
I have no influence over him; *you* can try,
But you will not succeed: she has some spell
That works from generation to generation.

MARY

Is Harry really going?

AGATHA

He is going.
But that is not my spell, it is none of my doing:
I have only watched and waited. In this world
It is inexplicable, the resolution is in another.

MARY

Oh, but it is the danger comes from another!

111

Can you not stop him? Cousin Agatha, stop him!
You do not know what I have seen and what I know!
He is in great danger, I know that, don't ask me,
You would not believe me, but I tell you I know.
You must keep him here, you must not let him leave.
I do not know what must be done, what can be done,
Even here, but elsewhere, everywhere, he is in danger.
I will stay or I will go, whichever is better;
I do not care what happens to me,
But Harry must not go. Cousin Agatha!

AGATHA

Here the danger, here the death, here, not elsewhere;
Elsewhere no doubt is agony, renunciation,
But birth and life. Harry has crossed the frontier
Beyond which safety and danger have a different meaning.
And he cannot return. That is his privilege.
For those who live in this world, this world only,
Do you think that I would take the responsibility
Of tempting them over the border? No one could, no one
    who knows.
No one who has the least suspicion of what is to be found
    there.
But Harry has been led across the frontier: he must
    follow;
For him the death is now only on this side,
For him, danger and safety have another meaning.
They have made this clear. And I who have seen them must
    believe them.

MARY

Oh! . . . so . . . *you* have seen them too!

AGATHA

We must all go, each in his own direction,
You, and I, and Harry. You and I,
My dear, may very likely meet again
In our wanderings in the neutral territory
Between two worlds.

MARY

                    Then you *will* help me!
You remember what I said to you this evening?
I knew that I was right: you made me wait for this —
Only for this. I suppose I did not really mean it
Then, but I mean it now. Of course it was much too late
Then, for anything to come for me: I should have known it;
It was all over, I believe, before it began;
But I deceived myself. It takes so many years
To learn that one is dead! So you must help me.
I will go. But I suppose it is much too late
Now, to try to get a fellowship?

AMY

                    So you will all leave me!
An old woman alone in a damned house.
I will let the walls crumble. Why should I worry
To keep the tiles on the roof, combat the endless weather,
Resist the wind? fight with increasing taxes
And unpaid rents and tithes? nourish investments
With wakeful nights and patient calculations
With the solicitor, the broker, agent? Why should I?
It is no concern of the body in the tomb
To bother about the upkeep. Let the wind and rain do that.
[*While* AMY *has been speaking,* HARRY *has entered, dressed
    for departure.*]

HARRY

But, mother, you will always have Arthur and John
To worry about: not that John is any worry —
The destined and the perfect master of Wishwood,
The satisfactory son. And as for me,
I am the last you need to worry about;
I have my course to pursue, and I am safe from normal
    dangers
If I pursue it. I cannot account for this
But it is so, mother. Until I come again.

AMY

If you go now, I shall never see you again.
[*Meanwhile* VIOLET, GERALD *and* CHARLES *have entered*]

CHARLES

Where is Harry going? What is the matter?

AMY

                            Ask Agatha.

GERALD

Why, what's the matter? Where is he going?

AMY

                            Ask Agatha.

VIOLET

I cannot understand at all. Why is he leaving?

AMY

                            Ask Agatha.

VIOLET

Really, it sometimes seems to me
That I am the only sane person in this house.
Your behaviour all seems to me quite unaccountable.
What *has* happened, Amy?

AMY

Harry is going away — to become a missionary.

HARRY

But . . . !

CHARLES

A missionary! that's never happened in our family!
And why in such a hurry? Before you make up your
     mind . . .

VIOLET

You can't really think of *living* in a tropical climate!

GERALD

There's nothing wrong with a tropical climate —
But you have to go in for some sort of training;
The medical knowledge is the first thing.
I've met with missionaries, often enough —
Some of them very decent fellows. A maligned profession.
They're sometimes very useful, knowing the natives,
Though occasionally troublesome. But you'll have to learn
     the language
And several dialects. It means a lot of preparation.

VIOLET

And you need some religious qualification!
I think you should consult the vicar . . .

115

GERALD

                              And don't forget
That you'll need various inoculations —
That depends on where you're going.

CHARLES

                              Such a thing
Has never happened in our family.

VIOLET

                              I cannot understand it.

HARRY

I never said that I was going to be a missionary.
I would explain, but you would none of you believe it;
If you believed it, still you would not understand.
You can't know why I'm going. You have not seen
What I have seen. Oh why should you make it so ridiculous
Just now? I only want, please,
As little fuss as possible. You must get used to it;
Meanwhile, I apologise for my bad manners.
But if you *could* understand you would be quite happy
        about it,
So I shall say good-bye, until we meet again.

GERALD

Well, if you are determined, Harry, we must accept it;
But it's a bad night, and you will have to be careful.
You're taking Downing with you?

HARRY

                              Oh, yes, I'm taking Downing.
You need not fear that I am in any danger

Of such accidents as happen to Arthur and John:
Take care of *them*. My address, mother,
Will be care of the bank in London until you hear from me.
Good-bye, mother.

AMY
Good-bye, Harry.

HARRY
Good-bye.

AGATHA
Good-bye.

HARRY
Good-bye, Mary.

MARY
Good-bye, Harry. Take care of yourself.
[*Exit* HARRY]

AMY
At my age, I only just begin to apprehend the truth
About things too late to mend: and that is to be old.
Nevertheless, I am glad if I can come to know them.
I always wanted too much for my children,
More than life can give. And now I am punished for it.
Gerald! you are the stupidest person in this room,
Violet, you are the most malicious in a harmless way;
I prefer your company to that of any of the others
Just to help me to the next room. Where I can lie down.
Then you can leave me.

GERALD
Oh, certainly, Amy.

VIOLET

I do not understand
A single thing that's happened.

[*Exeunt* AMY, VIOLET, GERALD]

CHARLES

It's very odd,
But I am beginning to feel, just beginning to feel
That there is something I *could* understand, if I were told it.
But I'm not sure that I want to know. I suppose I'm getting
old:
Old age came softly up to now. I felt safe enough;
And now I don't feel safe. As if the earth should open
Right to the centre, as I was about to cross Pall Mall.
I thought that life could bring no further surprises;
But I remember now, that I am always surprised
By the bull-dog in the Burlington Arcade.
What if every moment were like that, if one were awake?
You both seem to know more about this than I do.

[*Enter* DOWNING, *hurriedly, in chauffeur's costume*]

DOWNING

Oh, excuse me, Miss, excuse me, Mr. Charles:
His Lordship sent me back because he remembered
He thinks he left his cigarette-case on the table.
Oh, there it is. Thank you. Good night, Miss; good night,
Miss Mary; good night, Sir.

MARY

Downing, will you promise never to leave his Lordship
While you are away?

118

DOWNING

Oh, certainly, Miss;
I'll never leave him so long as he requires me.

MARY

But he will need you. You must never leave him.

DOWNING

You may think it laughable, what I'm going to say —
But it's not really strange, Miss, when you come to look
    at it:
After all these years that I've been with him
I think I understand his Lordship better than anybody;
And I have a kind of feeling that his Lordship won't need
    me
Very long now. I can't give you any reasons.
But to show you what I mean, though you'd hardly credit it,
I've always said, whatever happened to his Lordship
Was just a kind of preparation for something else.
I've no gift of language, but I'm sure of what I mean:
We most of us seem to live according to circumstance,
But with people like him, there's something inside them
That accounts for what happens to them. You get a feeling
    of it.
So I seem to know beforehand, when something's going to
    happen,
And it seems quite natural, being his Lordship.
And that's why I say now, I have a feeling
That he won't want me long, and he won't want anybody.

AGATHA

And, Downing, if his behaviour seems unaccountable

At times, you mustn't worry about that.
He is every bit as sane as you or I,
He sees the world as clearly as you or I see it,
It is only that he has seen a great deal more than that,
And we have seen them too — Miss Mary and I.

DOWNING

I understand you, Miss. And if I may say so,
Now that you've raised the subject, I'm most relieved —
If you understand my meaning. I thought that was the
     reason
We was off tonight. In fact, I half expected it,
So I had the car all ready. You mean them ghosts, Miss!
I wondered when his Lordship would get round to seeing
     them —
And so you've seen them too! They must have given you a
     turn!
They did me, at first. You soon get used to them.
Of course, I knew they was to do with his Lordship,
And not with me, so I could see them cheerful-like,
In a manner of speaking. There's no harm in *them*,
I'll take my oath. Will that be all, Miss?

AGATHA

That will be all, thank you, Downing. We mustn't keep
     you;
His Lordship will be wondering why you've been so long.
                    [*Exit* DOWNING. *Enter* IVY]

IVY

Where is Downing going? where is Harry?
Look. Here's a telegram come from Arthur;

[*Enter* GERALD *and* VIOLET]
I wonder why he sent it, after telephoning.
Shall I read it to you? I was wondering
Whether to show it to Amy or not.
                    [*Reads*]
'Regret delayed business in town many happy returns see
        you tomorrow many happy returns hurrah love Arthur.'
I mean, after what we know of what did happen,
Do you think Amy ought to see it?

                    VIOLET
                            No, certainly not.
You do not know what has been going on, Ivy.
And if you did, you would not understand it.
I do not understand, so how could you? Amy is not well;
And she is resting.

                    IVY
                Oh, I'm sorry. But can't you explain?
Why do you all look so peculiar? I think I might be allowed
To know what has happened.

                    AMY'S VOICE
                        Agatha! Mary! come!
The clock has stopped in the dark!
                    [*Exeunt* AGATHA *and* MARY. *Pause.*
                        Enter WARBURTON]

                    WARBURTON
Well! it's a filthy night to be out in.
That's why I've been so long, going and coming.
But I'm glad to say that John is getting on nicely;

It wasn't so serious as Winchell made out,
And we'll have him up here in the morning.
I hope Lady Monchensey hasn't been worrying?
I'm anxious to relieve her mind. Why, what's the trouble?
[*Enter* MARY]

MARY

Dr. Warburton!

WARBURTON

Excuse me.

[*Exeunt* MARY *and* WARBURTON]

CHORUS

We do not like to look out of the same window, and see
    quite a different landscape.
We do not like to climb a stair, and find that it takes us
    down.
We do not like to walk out of a door, and find ourselves back
    in the same room.
We do not like the maze in the garden, because it too closely
    resembles the maze in the brain.
We do not like what happens when we are awake, because
    it too closely resembles what happens when we are
    asleep.
We understand the ordinary business of living,
We know how to work the machine,
We can usually avoid accidents,
We are insured against fire,
Against larceny and illness,
Against defective plumbing,
But not against the act of God.

We know various spells and enchantments.
And minor forms of sorcery,
Divination and chiromancy,
Specifics against insomnia,
Lumbago, and the loss of money.
But the circle of our understanding
Is a very restricted area.
Except for a limited number
Of strictly practical purposes
We do not know what we are doing;
And even, when you think of it,
We do not know much about thinking.
What is happening outside of the circle?
And what is the meaning of happening?
What ambush lies beyond the heather
And behind the Standing Stones?
Beyond the Heaviside Layer
And behind the smiling moon?
And what is being done to us?
And what are we, and what are we doing?
To each and all of these questions
There is no conceivable answer.
We have suffered far more than a personal loss —
We have lost our way in the dark.

IVY

I shall have to stay till after the funeral: will my ticket to
   London still be valid?

GERALD

I do not look forward with pleasure to dealing with Arthur
   and John in the morning.

123

VIOLET

We must wait for the will to be read. I shall send a wire in
the morning.

CHARLES

I fear that my mind is not what it was — or was it? — and
yet I think that I might understand.

ALL

But we must adjust ourselves to the moment: we must do
the right thing.

[Exeunt]

[Enter, from one door, AGATHA *and* MARY, *and set a small
portable table. From another door, enter* DENMAN
*carrying a birthday cake with lighted candles, which she
sets on the table. Exit* DENMAN. AGATHA *and* MARY
*walk slowly in single file round and round the table,
clockwise. At each revolution they blow out a few candles,
so that their last words are spoken in the dark.]*

AGATHA

A curse is slow in coming
To complete fruition
It cannot be hurried
And it cannot be delayed

MARY

It cannot be diverted
An attempt to divert it
Only implicates others
At the day of consummation

124

AGATHA

A curse is a power
Not subject to reason
Each curse has its course
Its own way of expiation
           Follow follow

MARY

Not in the day time
And in the hither world
Where we know what we are doing
There is not its operation
           Follow follow

AGATHA

But in the night time
And in the nether world
Where the meshes we have woven
Bind us to each other
           Follow follow

MARY

A curse is written
On the under side of things
Behind the smiling mirror
And behind the smiling moon
           Follow follow

AGATHA

This way the pilgrimage
Of expiation
Round and round the circle

Completing the charm
So the knot be unknotted
The crossed be uncrossed
The crooked be made straight
And the curse be ended
By intercession
By pilgrimage
By those who depart
In several directions
For their own redemption
And that of the departed —
                    May they rest in peace.